THE SUN

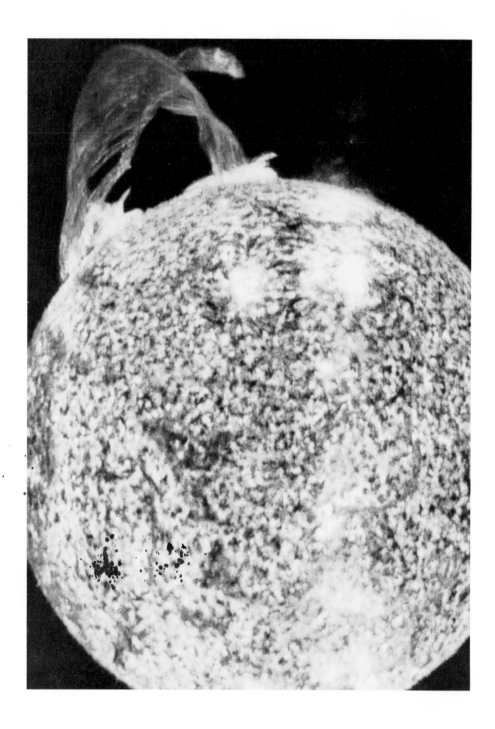

THE SUN
OUR NEIGHBORHOOD STAR

by David J. Darling

Illustrated by Jeanette Swofford

DILLON PRESS, INC.   MINNEAPOLIS, MINNESOTA

Photographs are reproduced through the courtesy of Don Andrews, the Department of Energy, Hale Observatories, Kitt Peak National Observatory, the National Aeronautics and Space Administration, and the Sacramento Peak Observatory.

Dillon Press, Inc., 242 Portland Avenue South
Minneapolis, Minnesota 55415

Printed in the United States of America

Library of Congress Cataloging in Publication Data

Darling, David J.
    The sun: our neighborhood star.

    Bibliography: p.
    Includes index.
    Summary: Explains what the sun is and how it produces such enormous amounts of energy.
    1. Sun—Juvenile literature. [1. Sun] I. Title.
QB521.5.D37   1984   523.7   84-12645
ISBN 0-87518-261-5 (lib. bdg.)

    2   3   4   5   6   7   8   9   10   91   90   89   88   87   86   85

Contents

Sun Facts

Age: More than 4½ billion years

Distance from Earth: *Average*—92,975,700 miles
(149,597,900 kilometers)
Closest—91,423,200 miles
(147,100,000 kilometers)
Farthest—94,530,800 miles
(152,100,000 kilometers)

Distance Across (Diameter): 865,100 miles
(1,392,000 kilometers)

Weight: 2 thousand trillion trillion tons

Temperature: *Surface*—11,000°F (6,000°C)
Core— 27,000,000°F (15,000,000°C)

Gravity at Sun's Surface: 28 times that of the earth

Chemical Makeup: *Hydrogen*—about 75 percent
Helium—almost 25 percent
Other—at least 70 other elements
make up the remaining 1 to 2
percent

Questions & Answers About the Sun

Q. How many times brighter is the sun than the full moon?
A. About 600,000 times.

Q. How long does it take light to go from the sun to the earth?
A. Just 8 1/3 minutes. Light is the fastest thing of all, traveling at more than 186,000 miles per second.

Q. How long does it take the sun to turn once around on its axis?
A. About 25 days.

Q. How many times heavier is the sun than the earth?
A. 332,946 times.

Q. Does this mean that the sun is a giant star?
A. No. In fact, scientists call the sun a "yellow dwarf." It is an ordinary star that only seems big and bright because it's so close.

Q. If you weighed 100 pounds on the earth, how much would you weigh on the sun?
A. Over 2¾ tons!

Q. What's the closest that a spacecraft has ever come to the sun?

A. About 28 million miles (45 million kilometers). The probe, *Helios 2*, came to within this distance of the sun's surface in 1976.

Q. Which substance was found in the sun before it was found on earth?

A. The gas, helium. Its name comes from the Greek word *helios*, meaning sun. Tell-tale dark lines in the sun's spectrum led to its discovery.

Q. What causes sunburn?

A. Ultraviolet rays from the sun. Some of these invisible rays manage to pass through the earth's atmosphere and reach the surface, where they can damage our skin.

Q. What is a rainbow?

A. A giant spectrum in the sky. It is caused by raindrops—each working like a tiny prism—that break up white light from the sun into its different colors.

Never look straight at the sun—
with or without a telescope.
It will hurt your eyes, and it may blind you.

1 A Sun to Live By

"And here is some late news. Leading scientists from around the world report that something strange is happening to our **sun.** The sun seems to be disappearing. Life-threatening effects are forecast for all the people of earth. More on this in our 10 P.M. report."

What a frightening story this would be to hear on the news—the sun disappearing! But could it ever happen? Could the sun ever just "switch off"? Happily the answer is no. The sun has been around for a very long time. It is in perfectly good health, and it will continue to be around for a very long time to come.

All the same, let's imagine what would happen if suddenly there were no sun. When we do, we realize how much we depend on the sun for nearly all we have.

Can you think of the two most important things that we get from the sun? Step outside on a warm summer's day and you'll have the answer: light and heat.

Without light from the sun, the earth would be a terribly gloomy place. Not only would there be no bright sun to light up our day, there would be no cheery moon at night. The moon shines simply by reflecting sunlight. Without a bright sun or moon in the sky, only the distant stars would be left to give a dim glow to our dark world.

Without light and heat from the sun, New York City would be a frozen, lifeless wasteland.

Food from the Sun

Do you think we could get used to living on a planet where it was always dark? Perhaps, but darkness would be the least of our worries. Without sunlight, all the green plants on earth would quickly die. For green plants—and that includes most plants—use sunlight, water, and air to make food and grow. The way in which they do this is called **photosynthesis.** *

Try an experiment with two small, healthy plants. They can be weeds, shoots of grass—anything with green leaves. Plant both carefully in good soil and give them some water. Now, put one of them in a sunny place such as a windowsill. Put the other in a place that's always dark; for example, a cupboard or a closet. Keep them both watered and watch what happens as the days go by.

*Words in **bold type** are explained in the glossary at the end of this book.

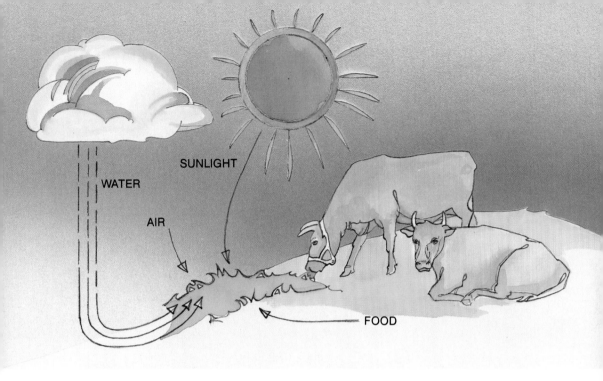

WATER

SUNLIGHT

AIR

FOOD

Green plants use sunlight, water, and air to make food and grow. Cows and many other animals depend on green plants for food. They, in turn, provide food for people and some other animals.

A dark world with no green plants would be a sad place. But green plants aren't the only living things that depend on the sun. Without these plants, all the animals that eat them would die, too! In fact, without sunlight, there would soon be no cows, no sheep, no type of land animal, bird, insect, or fish that depended on green plants for food.

All animals eat either plants or the flesh of other animals who have eaten plants. Without sunlight, then, all forms of life on earth—including people—would quickly die from lack of food.

Energy from the Sun

Sunlight is important in other ways, too. At night, for instance, how would you see to read this book? You would

Long ago, great forests covered the land. In swampy areas, plants died and sank into the mud. Over millions of years, the mud became thicker and heavier and formed the

turn on a light—an electric light. But where does the electricity to work the light come from? It comes from your local power plant. And how does the power plant make electricity? It probably makes it by burning coal, or oil, or natural gas. These are called **fossil fuels** and are all found in the ground, where they took a long time to form.

What have fossil fuels to do with sunlight? Before the age of the dinosaurs, great forests of strange trees, ferns, and other green plants covered the land. These forests needed sunlight to grow. In swampy areas, when the plants died, they sank into the mud. As the mud got thicker and heavier, the ancient plants were squashed harder. Over millions of years, they turned into coal.

In other places, countless tiny sea animals—which also depended on sunlight in some way for food—died

coal we use for energy today.

and fell to the seabed. There they were buried by thickening layers of mud and sand until, over time, they turned into oil or into natural gas.

What we are doing, then, when we burn coal, oil, or gas, is freeing the **energy** in sunlight that was trapped millions and millions of years ago by green plants! Strange as it may seem, most of our modern world runs on energy left to us long ago by the sun.

We know that fossil fuels took millions of years to form. Today, in our cars, planes, homes, and factories, we are using them up far faster than they can ever be replaced. What new forms of energy will we find to replace the disappearing fossil fuels? Many of them will, again, depend on the sun.

We are learning how to use the sun's energy directly

These solar collectors on the George A. Town Elementary School in Atlanta, Georgia, trap heat from the sun and help to heat and cool the school building.

At Sandia Laboratories in New Mexico, the U.S. Department of Energy tested the heating power of large solar collectors.

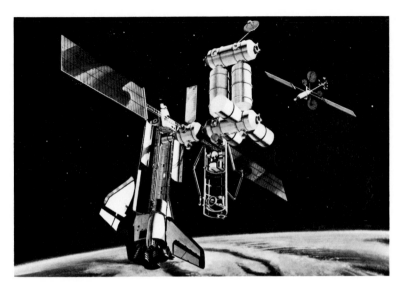

In this artist's picture of a future space station, solar panels gather the sun's energy to supply the station's power. A space shuttle is docked to the station to resupply it or change the crew.

to heat our buildings and to make electricity. Perhaps you have seen houses or schools in your neighborhood with **solar collectors** used for trapping heat from the sun. Most spacecraft use electricity made from sunlight by **solar cells.**

In the future, we might use giant curved mirrors—or groups of mirrors—to focus the sun's rays. In that way we may make a great deal of our electricity. But whether we use them wisely or not, light and heat from the sun will continue to pour onto the earth every day—just as they have for the last few billion years.

Weather from the Sun

The sun's heat is just as important to us as its light. Without heat from the sun, the earth would become

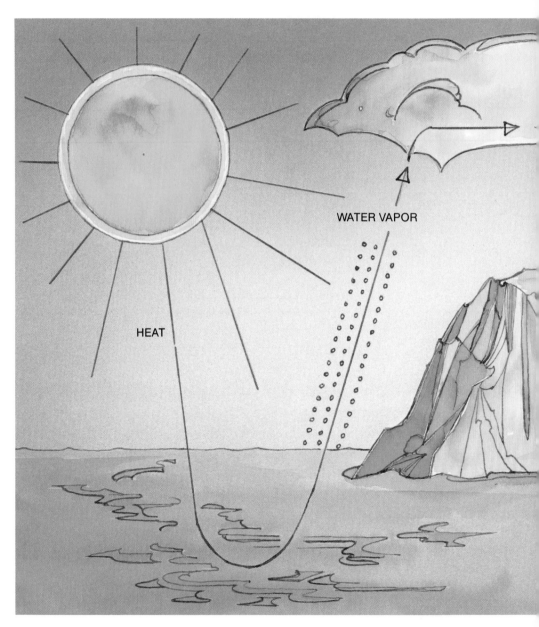

WATER VAPOR

HEAT

The sun heats the ocean and turns some of the water into water vapor. As the water vapor rises, it forms clouds, and the clouds produce rain.

RAIN

deadly cold. The oceans would freeze, and the temperature would drop below that of the worst Arctic winter.

Heat from the sun controls our weather, too. During the day, the sun's rays warm the land and ocean, which in turn warm the air above them. The warm air then moves both north and south to cooler regions, giving rise to winds.

As the sun heats the ocean, it also turns some of the water into water vapor. The mistlike vapor rises, cools, and eventually forms clouds. If the little water drops that make up the clouds grow big enough, they fall as rain.

Our weather, our fuels, our very lives depend so much on the sun. But what is the sun? Where did it come from? And what will happen to it in the distant future?

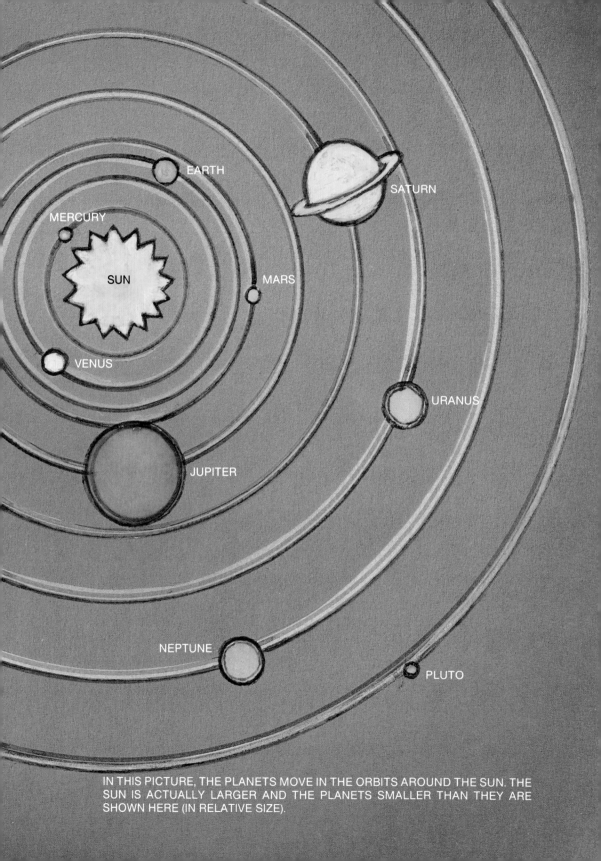

IN THIS PICTURE, THE PLANETS MOVE IN THE ORBITS AROUND THE SUN. THE SUN IS ACTUALLY LARGER AND THE PLANETS SMALLER THAN THEY ARE SHOWN HERE (IN RELATIVE SIZE).

2 Journey to the Center of the Sun

On a clear night, you can see hundreds of stars in the sky. During the day, though, you can see only one star—the sun.

The stars at night are all just tiny points of light. But the sun is a big yellow disk, extremely bright. Since the sun is a star, why does it look so much bigger and brighter than all the other stars? The answer is that, compared to other stars, the sun is very, very close. It is our "neighborhood star."

The Sun in Space

An express train, going 100 miles (160 kilometers) per hour, would take about 106 years to reach the sun. The same train would reach the moon in about 3 months and go around the earth in a little more than 10 days. But do you know how long it would take our train to get to the next nearest star after the sun? 28 million years! Compared with this distance, the sun is truly just a "space hop" away.

Actually, planet Earth is an inner member of the sun's family—the **solar system.** Earth orbits, or moves around, the sun, in a path that is roughly a circle, along with eight other planets. It takes Earth one year to go all

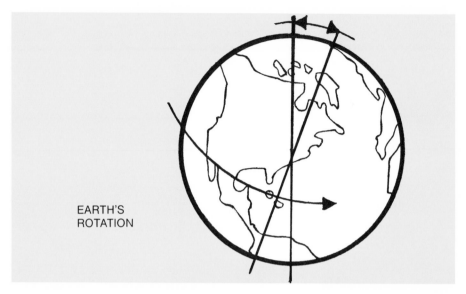

EARTH'S
ROTATION

This drawing shows the direction in which the earth rotates on its axis. As the earth spins like a top, its motion causes the place where you live to move from the day side to the night side.

the way around the sun. Our planet also spins on its **axis** like a top and takes one day to do a full turn in this way.

At night, our side of the earth is turned away from the sun. Then we see only the blackness of space, the stars, and sometimes the moon. During the day, though, our side of the earth is facing the sun. The sun's light makes the sky too bright for us to see any of the other stars.

Our Friendly, Neighborhood Star

Even at 93 million miles (150 million kilometers)—the distance from the sun to the earth—the sun looks big and bright. But can you imagine what the sun would be like close up? Its giant face is 865,000 miles (1,392,000 kilometers) in diameter—wider than a hundred earths. And, if we could set it on a scale, we would find that it

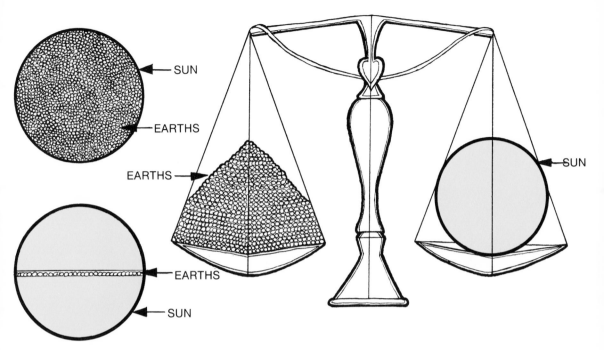

As you can see on the scale in this drawing, the sun is many times heavier than the earth. The pictures on the left show that it would take a large number of earths to equal the size of the sun.

weighed over five hundred times more than the rest of the solar system put together!

There are other things, too, apart from size and weight, that make the sun different from its family of planets. The sun is very hot. At its surface, the temperature is around 11,000°F (6,000°C)—hot enough to boil any metal. Deeper down, it is much hotter still.

Because it's so hot, the sun isn't a solid object like a planet. It is an enormous glowing ball of gas that gives off a great deal of light and heat of its own. Planets, moons, and smaller objects, on the other hand, shine only by reflecting sunlight. They have no light of their own.

This difference leads us to an important question. How does the sun make all that light and heat? Is it on fire? Is it perhaps exploding?

Inside the Sun

To find the answer, we will journey to the sun. We'll travel in an imaginary spaceship that can stand any temperature, no matter how high. And we'll take with us some useful gadgets for making measurements.

When we arrive, our first task is to find what the hot gas of the sun is made of. Using a special scoop, we gather up a sample and test it. Here are the results. At the sun's surface, three-quarters of the gas is **hydrogen,** one-quarter is **helium,** and only a tiny amount is anything else.

We can guess, then, that either hydrogen or helium must be the raw fuel from which the sun makes its light and heat. But exactly how does the sun "burn" its fuel? And where is the fiery furnace in which it makes the light and heat that give us life?

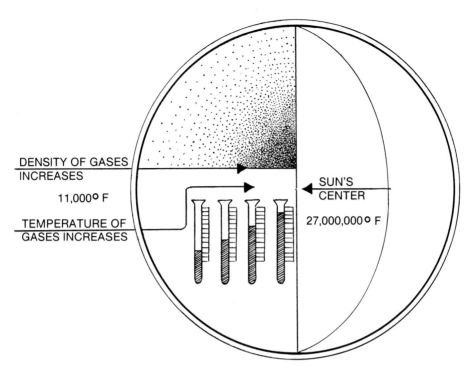

DENSITY OF GASES
INCREASES

11,000° F

TEMPERATURE OF
GASES INCREASES

SUN'S
CENTER

27,000,000° F

This drawing shows that the density and temperature of the sun increase greatly going from its surface toward its center.

Scientists know that the sun isn't burning like a fire. If it were, even though it is very big, it would have burnt to a dead cinder long ago. The sun has a much better way of making energy out of its gassy fuel.

To find out what it is, we must leave the sun's surface for a while and go below. Deeper and deeper we must go, towards the very core of our neighborhood star.

At the surface, the sun's gas is much thinner than the air we breathe on earth. But as we go deeper into the sun, the gas around us gets thicker. Its **density** rises.

The sun, because of its **gravity,** is always trying to pull itself together. Parts of the sun that are deep inside are squashed by the weight of the parts that are farther out. As we go deeper, the weight of the outside parts increases. The inside gas is squashed more and more, mak-

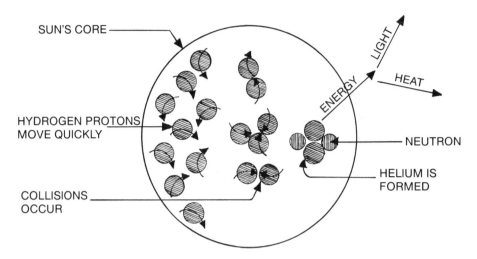

SUN'S CORE

HYDROGEN PROTONS
MOVE QUICKLY

COLLISIONS
OCCUR

ENERGY

LIGHT

HEAT

NEUTRON

HELIUM IS
FORMED

In this picture, fusion takes place in the sun's core as protons from hot hydrogen bump into each other and form helium.

ing it thicker. Gas right in the middle of the sun is so dense that a box full of it would weigh 12 times more than a box full of lead the same size!

Fusion Power

Something else, too, is unusual about the gas in the middle of the sun. It is very hot. Its temperature is at least 27,000,000°F (15,000,000°C).

Hot hydrogen in the sun's core is broken up into tiny pieces called **protons.** At the high temperature of the core, the protons dash around. They bump into each other a great deal, and sometimes they stick together.

When four protons have managed to stick together, they form a piece of helium. But they aren't exactly the same. Two protons have become **neutrons.** Together, all four pieces weigh a bit less than when they were all apart.

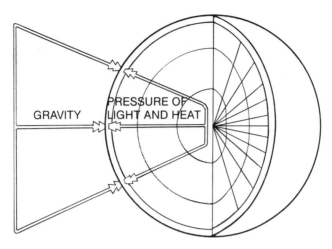

This drawing shows how the sun balances the inward force of gravity with its outward pressure of light and heat.

The bit that they lose is turned into energy—light and heat that, in time, escape from the sun's surface!

Here, then, in the core, is the sun's furnace. Pieces of hydrogen, called protons, sometimes strike each other, stick together, and build into pieces of helium. In this process, a tiny bit of matter is turned into a lot of energy that is given off by the sun as life-giving light and heat.

Scientists use the word **fusion** to describe how the sun makes energy. Protons are fused to form helium. Slowly, the middle of the sun is losing hydrogen and gaining helium. But it will take a very long time for the sun to run out of its hydrogen fuel.

While fusion goes on in its core, the sun has a way to stop itself from being squeezed by gravity. The sun stays the same size by balancing its inward force of gravity with its outward **pressure** of light and heat.

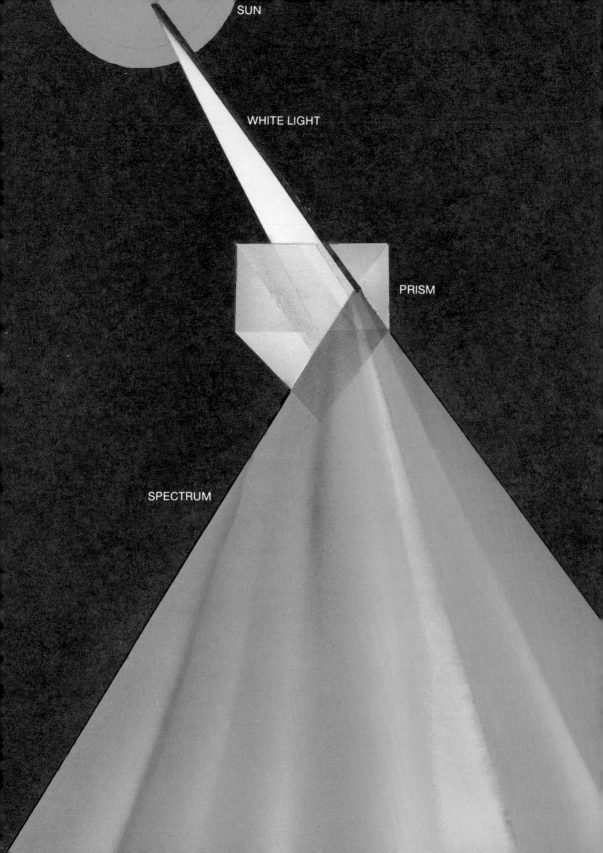

SUN

WHITE LIGHT

PRISM

SPECTRUM

3 Sun-Watching

Of course, we can't actually see inside the sun. No real spacecraft has ever gone there, for it would be melted on approach by the tremendous heat. How, then, are we able to learn so much about our neighborhood star?

One way is breaking the "secret code" contained in sunlight. Amazingly enough, even the tiniest sunbeam carries with it a great deal of information about the place in the sun where it came from.

Secrets of the Spectrum

If we pass sunlight through a glass triangle—a **prism**—we find that the light is made, not just of one color, but of many. What looks like white sunlight is really a mixture of all the colors of the rainbow. The split-up sunlight forms a **spectrum** of colors stretching from red through orange, yellow, green, blue, indigo, to violet.

Using a special instrument, called a **spectroscope**, scientists can get a much clearer look at the spectrum of sunlight. In this way they can uncover something even more surprising about it. Not only is the sun's spectrum made of many colors, but it is also crossed by hundreds and hundreds of dark, narrow lines. These are called **Fraunhofer lines** in honor of one of the first scientists who noticed them.

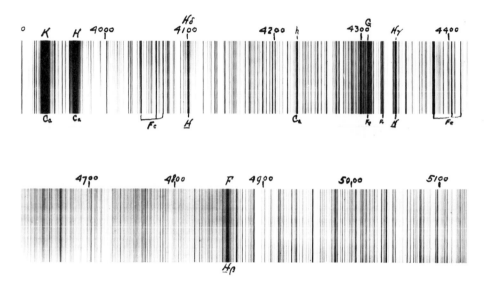

The Fraunhofer lines in this spectrum of sunlight carry the secret code that reveals how hot and dense the surface of the sun is.

The Fraunhofer lines carry the secret code in sunlight. They are made by substances high up in the sun that absorb light coming from deeper down. By studying these lines, scientists have learned what the outside of the sun is made of and how hot and dense it is.

The Sun Seen from Earth

Another way we can learn about the sun is simply by looking at it. But how can we do this safely? If we gazed straight at the sun or tried to view it through an ordinary telescope, it would be so bright that it would blind us.

To view the sun safely, scientists use special **solar telescopes.** These have mirrors that track the sun across the sky, collect its light, and form an image, or picture, of its brilliant disk on a large, flat viewing table.

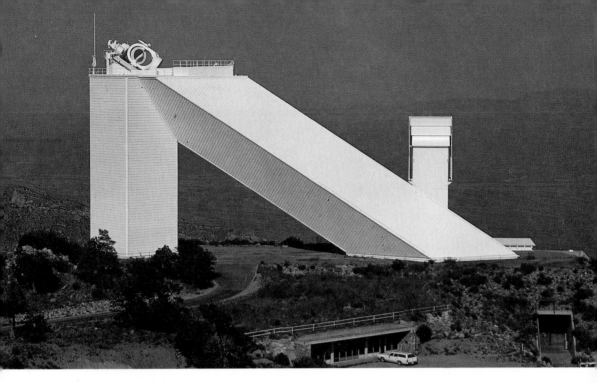

The McMath solar telescope near Tucson, Arizona, uses a mirror 5 feet (1.5 meters) in diameter to track the sun across the sky. Sunlight streams 480 feet (146 meters) down its shaft to the mirror.

What is it we see when we look at the sun in this way? It is the sun's bright surface, the **photosphere,** a bubbling, boiling, bursting brew. Seen through a solar telescope, the sun's surface is always shifting, always alive with movement.

There are, for instance, tiny freckles that cover the entire surface of the sun. Scientists call these **granules** and believe they are caused by hot gases that well up from deeper in the sun, cool, and then fall back down again. The pattern of granules presents a dotlike, ever-changing picture.

Sunspots are much larger and darker spots on the face of the sun. They may last a week or more and may be big enough to swallow several earths.

A sunspot is an area of the sun's surface that has

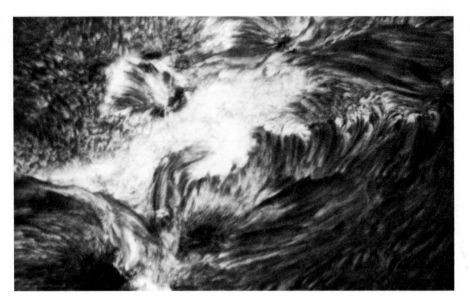

In this close-up photograph of the sun, details of a small active region show the granules caused by hot gases from within.

been made a little cooler than its surroundings. Because the center of a sunspot is cooler than the rest of the sun's surface, it looks dark. But a sunspot is still quite hot— around 7,000°F (4,000°C)—and, by itself, a large one would look as bright as the full moon!

Sunspots are formed when the sun's **magnetic field** bursts up through the photosphere. Since the magnetic field then usually loops back around into the surface, a second sunspot may be formed. These loops are the reason sunspots often occur in pairs.

Sometimes there may be no sunspots for several weeks. At other times the sun's face seems peppered with them. Then their position changes daily as the sun slowly turns on its axis. Over a period of years, though, the average number of sunspots gradually goes up, hits a peak,

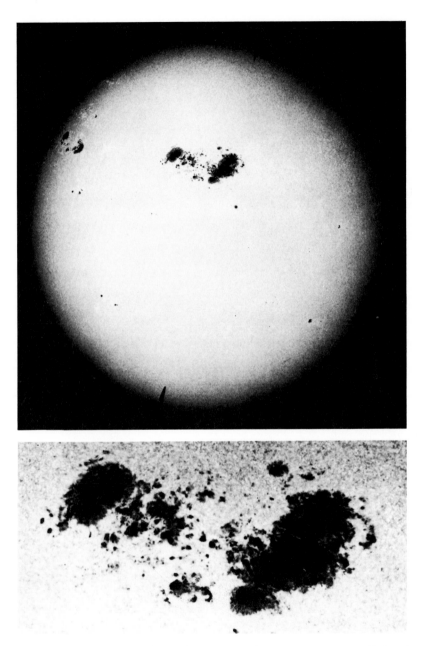

The photograph of the sun above shows a very large sunspot group. Below is a close-up of the same sunspot group as photographed on April 7, 1947.

and then gradually falls off again. The sunspot peaks happen about every eleven years, and the whole pattern of their change is known as the **sunspot cycle.**

The Sun Eclipsed

The bright surface of the sun is called the photosphere. But this fiery area isn't where the sun ends and "outer space" begins. The sun also has a huge atmosphere—a layer of gases outside the photosphere—that we can't usually see.

Only at a very special time can we get a good view of the sun's much dimmer atmosphere. It is during a **total eclipse** of the sun.

You may have noticed that the moon and the sun seem to be about the same size in the sky. (In fact, the

On June 8, 1918, in Green River, Wyoming, a photographer captured the sun at the exact moment of a total eclipse.

moon is really very much smaller and closer to us.) Once in a great while, the moon passes exactly between the sun and the earth. Then, from some parts of the earth, the sun's bright disk is completely blotted out by the moon.

During a few minutes of a total eclipse, we get a thrilling glimpse of what is going on above the surface of the sun. For a short time, just at the start and at the end of the total eclipse, we see a thin, pinkish, curved ring around the edge of the sun. This is the **chromosphere**—the bottom part of the sun's atmosphere. The chromosphere is like a bubbling foam of gases, a few thousand miles deep, thrown up by the "sea" of the photosphere.

During the middle of the eclipse, we see a beautiful, glowing **corona**—the top part of the sun's atmosphere. Although the corona is made of only very thin, very hot

35

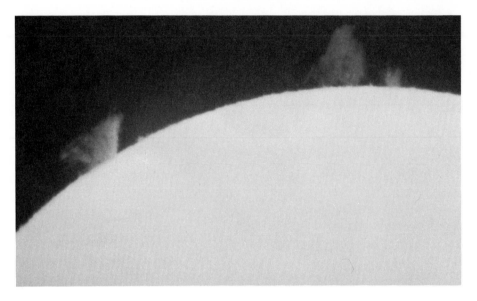

This prominence of the sun, 205,000 miles high, was photographed in violet light on July 2, 1957.

gases, it is huge. It stretches more than a million miles out from the sun in every direction!

Total eclipses also provide us with marvelous views of **prominences.** These are great clouds of slightly thicker gas that form in the corona and then rain down onto the sun's surface. They look like giant flaming tongues.

Another, rarer type of prominence—the **eruptive prominence**—is caused by gas bursting out of the sun's surface. In fact, it is just one of the ways in which the sun can shoot matter into space.

From Sun to Earth

A strange kind of wind—the **solar wind**—carries about one million tons of the sun into space every second! Some of the tiny, fast-moving particles in the solar wind

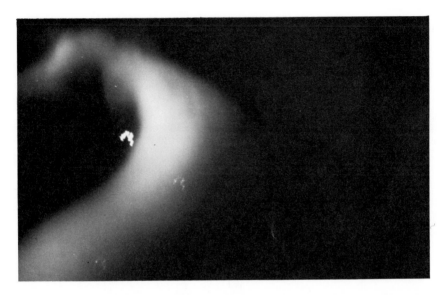

During the night of January 19, 1968, a camera aboard a specially equipped jet plane took this picture of an Arctic aurora. From top to bottom, the aurora is more than 100 miles high.

reach earth and get trapped in the magnetic field that stretches all the way around our planet. Just a few of the solar wind particles then manage to leak out of the magnetic field at the poles. They rise into the air and cause a wonderful shimmering glow in the sky. This is how **aurora** are made.

The solar wind blows especially hard following a **solar flare**—an explosion of the sun's surface that sends a sudden burst of particles into space. Solar flares cause **magnetic storms** around the earth. For a while, the aurora become brighter, and radios and compasses behave in an odd way.

Scientists know of other things, too, that the sun gives off. **Radio waves** and **X rays** reach earth from the sun's surface. And huge armies of strange, ghostly parti-

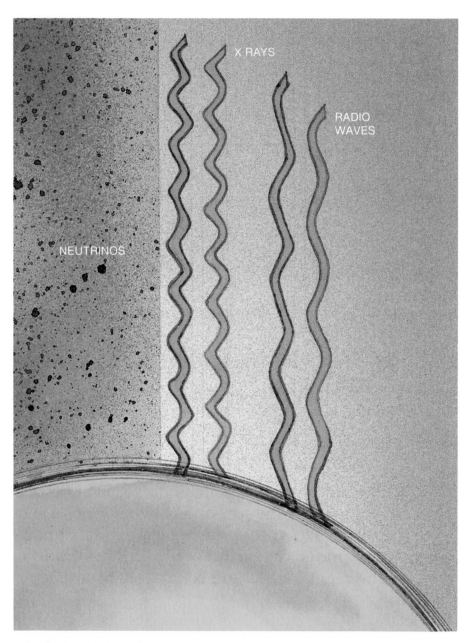

Radio waves, X rays, and tiny particles called neutrinos are given off by the sun and reach or pass through the earth.

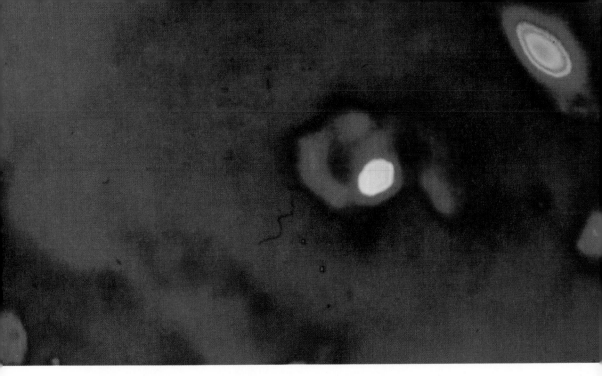

During the *Skylab 2* mission, scientist-astronaut Joseph Kerwin took this X-ray photograph of the sun. In the photo the red regions are the faintest and the white, the brightest, in the sun's corona.

cles, called **neutrinos,** march out to meet us from the sun's core.

By building special instruments on earth, and by launching others on satellites, we can study what the "radio sun," the "X ray sun," and even the "neutrino sun" look like. In this way, we can get a better understanding of how our neighborhood star works.

PLANETS FORMED

SUN FORMED

AN ARTIST'S VIEW OF HOW THE SOLAR SYSTEM WAS FORMED

4 The Birth and Death of the Sun

It's hard to imagine that the sun has not always been the way it is today. Yet there was a time, in the distant past, when the sun did not exist.

More than 5 billion years ago, there was no sun, no earth, no solar system at all. There was, instead, just a huge, thin cloud of gas and dust slowly turning and drifting through space.

Gradually, the cloud became smaller. Because of its own gravity, it pulled itself together. At the same time, it began to get hotter and denser.

By about 5 billion years ago, nearly all the cloud's gas was packed into a big, fuzzy ball at the center of the cloud. Then a very important thing happened. Deep inside the ball, the temperature rose high enough for fusion to start. Hydrogen began to turn into helium, making light and heat. What had been a ball of gas became a star: the sun.

But there was more to come. Not all of the gas had been used in making the sun. Some of it settled into a flat, pancake-shaped cloud that now circled the newborn star. Slowly, from this cloud, the planets, moon, and other members of the sun's family formed. Since then the solar system has not changed.

What will happen to the sun in the future? For bil-

The Orion Nebula is an example of an actual star-forming region. This photograph was taken by one of the large telescopes at the Kitt Peak National Observatory.

This is an artist's view of how the earth might look when the sun becomes a red giant.

lions of years, it will carry on "burning" hydrogen fuel in its core. Although the sun uses up around 5 million tons of hydrogen every second, it still has enough left in its core to last for another 5 billion years or so.

When it finally does run out of fuel, though, something very odd will happen to the sun. It will swell up to many times its current size and become what is known as a **red giant.**

The outer layers of the sun will grow to swallow up, in turn, the planets Mercury and Venus. They may even reach out as far as Earth. Then, the surface of our planet will be scorched, and its oceans boiled dry.

As a red giant, the sun might be able to exist for a few more million years. During this time it will shed matter quite quickly. The solar wind will strengthen to a solar

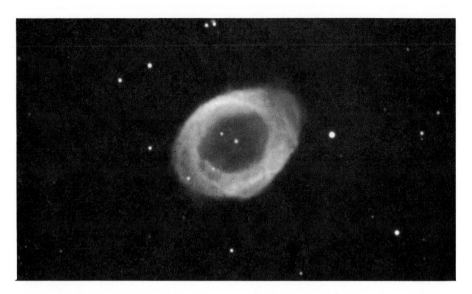

When the sun becomes a planetary nebula, it may look something like the Ring Nebula. This picture of a planetary nebula was taken at the Kitt Peak National Observatory.

gale. Finally, the sun may blow off most of its outer layers as a bright shell of gas called a **planetary nebula.**

All that will be left behind is a very hot, dense core. The sun, in fact, will have become a **white dwarf**—a star no bigger than the earth. Gradually, over millions of years, even this small star will cool. The sun will end its days quietly as a dimming ember in space.

Before this happens, human beings may have learned how to travel to other stars. We may be able to make our home on a planet around a friendlier star. But perhaps we will leave behind a robot probe to watch the final fate of our old neighborhood star.

Appendix A:
Discover For Yourself

1. *Make a sun-earth-moon model*

On a sheet of paper, trace the large circle *A* and the box *B*. Trace, too, the very small circle and the tiny dot inside box *B*. (Use the shapes on page 48)

Now, cut out the large circle and the box. In your yard or local park, place the large circle 36 feet (11 meters) away from the box. Perhaps you could borrow a long tape measure and get a friend to help you do this.

The large circle represents the sun. The very small circle in the box represents the earth, and the tiny dot—also in the box—the moon.

Your model shows just how big the sun is compared with the earth or moon, and how far away it is. If you like, try rolling a ball about two-thirds of an inch every second from the sun towards the earth. In your model, the ball represents a ray of light—traveling at over 186,000 miles per second!

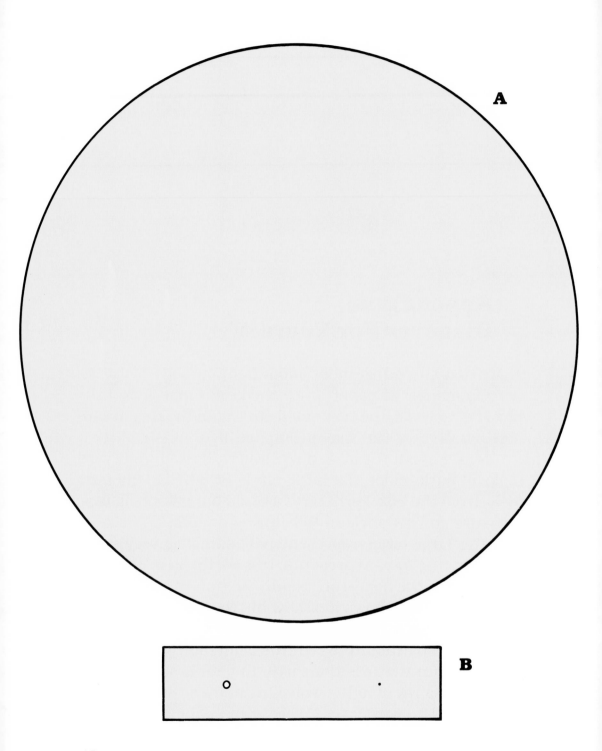

A

B

48

2. *Find out how a solar collector works*

Cut out a square of aluminum foil, another of black card, and yet another of white card. Place all three squares in a very sunny spot and leave them for several minutes. Now, put your hand on each of them in turn. What do you notice? Which color traps the most heat from the sun?

Look at the picture on page 16. Better still, visit a building in your neighborhood that has solar collectors fitted. What color are the collectors? Why are they set at an angle to the ground? Will this help them to gather more heat from the sun?

3. Spot an eclipse of the sun

Total eclipses are quite rare, and there will not be another that can be seen from the United States until the next century. Partial eclipses or annular eclipses—in which a part of the sun's bright face still shows behind the moon—are a little more common.

Below is a list of all the solar eclipses that can be seen from the earth until 1999. Perhaps you'll be lucky enough to be in the right place, at the right time, to see one of them.

Eclipses of the Sun: 1984-1999

Date	Places From Which It Can Be Seen	Type
Nov 22, 1984	East Indies, Pacific	Total
May 19, 1985	Arctic	Partial
Nov 12, 1985	Pacific, Antarctic	Total
Apr 9, 1986	Antarctic	Partial
Oct 3, 1986	Atlantic	Total
Mar 29, 1987	Argentina, Central Africa, Atlantic, Indian Ocean	Total
Sep 23, 1987	Russia, China, Pacific	Annular
Mar 18, 1988	East Indies, Pacific, Indian Ocean	Total
Mar 7, 1989	Arctic	Partial
Aug 31, 1989	Antarctic	Partial
Jan 26, 1990	Antarctic	Annular
Jul 22, 1990	Finland, Russia, Pacific	Total
Jan 15, 1991	Australia, New Zealand, Pacific	Annular
Jul 11, 1991	Mexico, Brazil, Pacific	Total
Jan 4, 1992	Central Pacific	Annular

Date	Places From Which It Can Be Seen	Type
Jun 30, 1992	Atlantic	Total
Dec 24, 1992	Arctic	Partial
May 21, 1993	Arctic	Partial
Nov 13, 1993	Antarctic	Partial
May 10, 1994	United States, Canada, Mexico, Pacific	Annular
Nov 3, 1994	Brazil, Peru, Atlantic	Total
Apr 29, 1995	Peru, Atlantic, Pacific	Annular
Oct 24, 1995	Iran, India, East Indies, Pacific	Total
Apr 17, 1996	Antarctic	Partial
Oct 12, 1996	Arctic	Partial
Mar 9, 1997	Russia, Arctic	Total
Sep 2, 1997	Antarctic	Partial
Feb 26, 1998	Atlantic, Pacific	Total
Aug 22, 1998	East Indies, Pacific, Indian Ocean	Annular
Feb 16, 1999	Australia, Pacific, Indian Ocean	Annular
Aug 11, 1999	England, France, Turkey, India, Atlantic	Total

Appendix B:
Amateur Astronomy Groups
in the United States,
Canada, and Great Britain

For information or resource materials about the subjects covered in this book, contact your local astronomy group, science museum, or planetarium. You may also write to one of the national amateur astronomy groups listed below.

United States
The Astronomical League
Donald Archer,
  Executive Secretary
P.O. Box 12821
Tucson, Arizona 85732

American Association of
  Variable Star Astronomers
187 Concord Avenue
Cambridge, Massachusetts 02138

Great Britain
Junior Astronomical Society
58 Vaughan Gardens
Ilford
Essex IG1 3PD England

British Astronomical Assoc.
Burlington House
Piccadilly
London W1V 0NL England

Canada
The Royal Astronomical Society of Canada
La Société Royale d'Astronomie du Canada
Rosemary Freeman, Executive Secretary
136 Dupont Street
Toronto, Ontario M5R 1V2

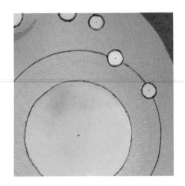

Glossary

atmosphere—the layer of gases above the surface of a star or planet

aurora—glowing bands of light in the sky caused by particles from the sun that hit the earth's atmosphere. Aurora are especially bright near the poles

axis—the imaginary line about which a spinning object (such as the sun or earth) seems to turn

billion—a thousand million. Written as 1,000,000,000

chromosphere—the bottom layer of the sun's atmosphere. It is a few thousand miles thick and lies between the photo-sphere and the corona

core—the small heavy, central part of a star or planet

corona—the top layer of the sun's atmosphere. It is about a million miles high, and is made of very thin, very hot gases

density—a measure of how concentrated an object is. It tells how much mass there is in a given volume

eclipse—the blocking of light from a bright object by something that passes in front of it. Eclipses of the sun are caused by the moon moving between the sun and the earth. See *total eclipse*

energy—the ability to be active or do work. There are many forms of energy. Those made inside the sun include radio waves, X rays, light, and electricity or electrical energy

eruptive prominence—a type of *prominence*—a cloud of hot gas—that bursts out of the sun's surface

fossil fuel—a substance made long ago, from dead plants or small animals, from which we now get energy. Fossil fuels—coal, oil, and natural gas—are really "stored sunlight"

Fraunhofer lines—dark, narrow lines in the sun's spectrum. They are caused by substances in the sun's atmosphere that absorb light coming from the sun's surface. See *spectrum*

fusion—the way in which the sun makes energy by turning hydrogen into helium

granule—a speckle on the sun's surface made by hot gasses that rise, cool, and then fall back into the sun again.

gravity—the force by which all objects pull on all other objects. Gravity is what makes the planets go around the sun. It is also what holds an object, like the sun, together

helium—a gas. The second

lightest substance in the universe and the second most commonly found in the sun

hydrogen—a gas. The lightest substance of all and the most common in the sun. It is the "fuel" from which the sun makes its heat and light

magnetic field—a region in which a force of magnetism can be felt. The sun and the earth, for example, both have magnetic fields

magnetic storm—a disturbance in the earth's magnetic field caused by a solar flare. During a magnetic storm, radios, TVs, and compasses are affected

million—a thousand thousand. Written as 1,000,000

neutrino—a tiny particle made during fusion in the center of the sun. Almost nothing can stop a neutrino, and billions and billions of them pass all the way through the earth every second

neutron—a tiny particle made during fusion in the sun's core. Two neutrons and two protons form pieces of helium in the sun

photosphere—the bright surface of the sun

photosynthesis—the process by which green plants make food from

sunlight, water, and air

planet—a large object that, along with comets, meteors, and asteroids, moves around a star. The sun has nine planets in its family, one of which is the earth

planetary nebula—a bright ring, or shell, of gas that is thrown off by some stars in their old age.

pressure—a force that pushes steadily on a certain area or surface

prism—a solid block of glass, with triangular ends, that can split white light into its rainbow of colors

prominence—a bright cloud of gas in the sun's atmosphere

proton—a tiny particle. Protons, from split-up

hydrogen, fuse in the sun's core and give off great amounts of energy

radio waves—weak, invisible waves of energy that, like light and heat, are given off by many different objects

red giant—a kind of star that, in its old age, has grown very big. At its surface, a red giant is cool and glows with a reddish light

solar—to do with the sun. Solar comes from the Roman word, *sol*, meaning sun

solar cell—a device used for making electricity from sunlight. Solar cells are

often used to power
spacecraft

solar collector—a flat box,
with a glass top and a black-
painted bottom, that uses
sunlight to heat water in
pipes that pass through it

solar flare—a sudden
explosion, or release of
energy, at the sun's surface
that sends a burst of
particles into space. A solar
flare can cause a magnetic
storm around the earth

solar system—the sun
plus all of the objects that
go around it, including:
planets, moons, asteroids,
meteors, and comets

solar telescope—a special
kind of telescope that
scientists use for looking at
the sun

solar wind—a force that
carries about one million
tons of tiny, fast-moving
particles from the sun into
space every second. Some of
the particles are trapped in
the earth's magnetic field
and later leak out at the
poles, where they cause a
shimmering, colorful glow
known as aurora

spectroscope—an
instrument used for
studying a spectrum. It is
much better than a simple
prism at showing all of a
spectrum's fine detail

spectrum—the rainbow
of colors obtained by
splitting up white light

star—a very large ball of
gases that shines by its own
light and heat

sun—our nearest star and the one around which the earth revolves

sunspot—an area of the sun's surface—thousands of miles across—that looks dark because it is a little cooler than its surroundings.

sunspot cycle—the period, and also the way, in which the number of sunspots goes from very high, to very low, and back to very high again

total solar eclipse—a complete blocking of the sun's bright disk by the moon. It happens quite rarely, lasts only a few minutes, and can be seen only from certain parts of the earth

white dwarf—a very small, very hot star that has stopped making energy in its core. A star becomes a white dwarf after it has gone through its red giant stage

X rays—very powerful, invisible waves of energy. Although they are similar to light and heat, X rays are made only in special places, such as the atmospheres of stars

Suggested Reading

Branley, Franklyn M. *The End of the World.* New York:
    Thomas Y. Crowell, 1974.
In pictures and words, describes what the last years on
Earth may be like as the sun grows to become a red giant.

Catherall, Ed. *Solar Power.* Morristown, N.J.: Silver Burdett,
    1982.
Describes simple experiments that you can do to find out
what solar energy is and how it works.

Lampton, Christopher. *Fusion: The Eternal Flame.* New
    York: Franklin Watts, 1982.
Talks about what fusion is, how the sun uses it to make
light and heat, and how we may harness fusion ourselves in
the future for making energy. This book also takes us into
the far future of space travel and of the universe itself.

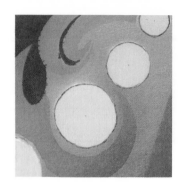

 Index